AND LUCKIER

And Luckier

Poems by
Leatha Kendrick

Accents Publishing • Lexington, Kentucky • 2020

Copyright © 2020 by Leatha Kendrick
All rights reserved

Printed in the United States of America

Accents Publishing
Editor: Katerina Stoykova
Cover Painting: *Sweet Afternoon* by Lynn Winter

Library of Congress Control Number: 2020934968
ISBN: 978-1-936628-56-8
First Edition

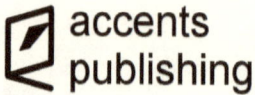

Accents Publishing is an independent press for brilliant voices. For a catalog of current and upcoming titles, please visit us on the Web at

www.accents-publishing.com

CONTENTS

I. Home Fires

Your Fear / 3
Next World / 4
Persephone Opens Another Bottle of Red / 5
Dream Shop / 6
Domicile / 7
House Beautiful / 8
Tableaux / 9
Poem for a Daughter, I / 10
Winter Solstice on George Branch, 2013 / 11
No Place Like Home / 12
That's Good / 13
Before the Bloom / 14
Question Poem / 16
Eviction / 17
There Was a Door / 18

II. Broken, Various, Inscrutable

The Next Knot / 23
Another April / 24
Out the Door / 26
Consider the Measure of a Step / 27
Knobbed / 31
Still Longing for the Divine / 32
Poem for a Daughter, II / 34
Mortal Coil / 35
Thanksgiving in a Year of Flood and Fire / 36
The Absentee Nana Fixes Her Solitary Lunch / 37
Our Own / 38
What Does a Heaven Require? / 39
Diorama / 41
Nights at Home after the Surgery / 43
How to Go On / 45

III. Unasked-for Singing

After Rain / 49
Poem Without a Gazelle / 50
Ode to my Left Knee / 51
Naming It / 53
Poem for a Daughter, III / 54
At the Gate / 55
The Warp / 56
Between Heaven and Earth / 57
Lady Proteus / 58
Reinvention / 59
Morning Shift with Canine / 61
Salt / 62
And Luckier / 63
In Your Pocket / 65
We Are Here / 66

Acknowledgments / 67

About the Author / 69

I. Home Fires

YOUR FEAR

Now ask yourself—who might it serve that you
would grow downhearted? What do you choose
to see? What will your seeing make? The "news"
selected and relayed, mirrored and soon
a billion times its weight, weighs on the mind
that seeks it out. What is the new? The breath
just drawn, the thought not yet enfleshed, the kind
word being said, the stars that press unseen
overhead. "It is the unforeseen
upon which," Poe said, "we must calculate
most largely." Impossible to separate
misery and joy—the living edge of mystery.
Time's unfolding, dauntless, holds you dear.
The universe has no need of your fear.

NEXT WORLD

Tell an unborn child
there is dancing here,
a blaze of scarlet leaves
at autumn, seas that whisper
to the sand, vermillion rose-
gold skies at evening.

I dance, he'll say. His legs,
flexed, test a wall.
I hear the ocean pulse,
drift in warm waters,
gaze on ruby skies
bright and filtered.
Sleep, dream. I know
that other world—
how it must be.

Tell him galaxies, wind,
houses, lightning,
lovers' fingers, dinner's
warm steams rising,
a flower. *Yes, yes,*
he'll say. *I know.*

PERSEPHONE OPENS ANOTHER BOTTLE OF RED

After all this time the signs hovered clear enough—blank sky of reverie cut by raven wings, her uneasy urge to leave the earth—the earth uneven giving way beneath the blood-red bloom she had to have. Hades reaching through to claim her. His hands all smoke and stone grown tight around her wrist tow her headfirst through the bottle's neck into that huge roofed dark. Oh right beforehand she'd crave that skyless place where even as queen she might sit dead in her chair, her gifts forgotten shades. All she wanted was away from thought's steady calcite drip—insistent beat coagulating the blue vault of sky, hardening the riotous fields, the branch heavy with fruits. And waking, after, robed in her own dank odor, dying to dig her way out, certain she can't—only the slip of time keeps breath treading its old passageways, circling back to a notion of light and air. To the heart's open eye.

DREAM SHOP
—a triolet

The grocery cart's shrunk. I didn't pick this
child-sized one I find I am hunched over.
What have I eaten? How did I miss
when the cart shrank? I wouldn't pick this
Nordic store's bright simple birch cases,
exotic fruits, wooden, under cloth covers.
Everything's shrunken. I didn't pick this.
Child-sized, wandering, all hunched over.

DOMICILE

      House of water
                      bone and cell.
Terra
    mostly   incognita
       more microbe
              than me,
running on its
        gut. Kept
             sensate by God
  knows what
        bright wick
at its core.

     In every room
           a spiral
                 staircase.
        A scaffold
spun of touches
        into joining,
  it grows
     new being
           in a warm
and inward sea.
        Cytoplasmic sac

    we're stitched   into

so long as
       breath threads
  us here.
          Country past whose
     borders
it is impossible
      to stray.

HOUSE BEAUTIFUL

The twigs of every bush along the walk,
every stick of furniture in rooms flat
and glassy as Narcissus's pool, each vase
and lamp and magazine arranged
with a casual precision—"casual
precision," an oxymoron, ought
to be a clue. Step too far in,
the net contracts. You're set to be digested
by *Architectural Digest's* dream rooms,
dissolved into *house*. Shelter

as dress. Evolution
of the hearth, the hot red maw
that ground women's lives,
masticated hours
and days. Thought lost
to "keeping." Escapes small
and close: nursing a child,
a garden, sometimes needlework
at the evening window.
As years devolve,
perhaps the heavy
gloss of a magazine.

TABLEAUX

When I was young I thought our house must send out scenes
of quiet light, of meals and table, lamps and after-supper rest—
a pantomime, a shadow show of happiness. I wanted this,
just warm enough with life, just cool enough with regimented
bliss, to announce we'd found out how to be a happy family.
Never mind the heated words, the fires of want in each of us,
the jealousies and Mother at the stove, her icy back that walled us
out, her barbed tongue, we had the house, upright white clapboard,
tall windows spooling light onto the drive,
the back door unlocked waiting for our dad, the table set.

The tableau is what we went for, getting the story straight,
playing our parts: good daughter, rebel sister, quiet brother,
and the baby boy escaping every playpen, upending order.
Mother in charge, plucky heroine, burdened but up to it,
smiling even (oh the cost of that apparent ease, her grip
on the stirring spoon, the hairbrush, her great, grim
impatience). The father not quite there, lord and
scapegoat, benevolent, distant, wreathed with his
intermittent flashes, like lightnings from Olympus.

Give up your icy back,
embrace your stiffened shoulders,
even the true/false scene
of (un)happiness,
all of us
together in those hours,
discontent, but home.

POEM FOR A DAUGHTER, I

This hard clear thing. I thought it was only air. I thought
when you were here we would reach through it. It is only bone
and living skin that separates us, that and silence. I imagined
it a bubble to disperse at our touch. You move
from room to room, lovely as the iridescent swimmers past
foot-thick plate glass—false mermaids straining not
to breathe. What holds us apart is rigid—the cover
of a lake at midwinter. I cannot get past its cold.
Hard as magnets, faced positive to positive one minute,
negatives head-on the next, we force each other away.
We pass through rooms I thought we'd always have,
though we chased life outside of them. When did we
leave off talking? One true word, one sentence.
What did I want? What did I want, even then?
but that? Your slim back under my hand, your ear.

WINTER SOLSTICE ON GEORGE BRANCH, 2013

Remember. The light drew down like this,
blocked by the ridge in winter days
of soup and chatter at the table, a bliss
deep and unselfconscious. Costumes, plays,
homework, meets. Talk and music thronged
the minivan, the living room—rich
broth, it distilled the light we longed
for. Light suffused our faces, tuned the pitch

we harmonized in rounds of Deck the Halls,
sung raucous in the car. The shortest day
rolled past with us inside it. Our separate ways
launched even then in that house astride the fall
and rise of ancient mountains, the wash of earth
toward creek, the hollow we would each desert.

NO PLACE LIKE HOME

1.

She'd wanted out—of the hills—of the car—of the kitchen—of ~~her life~~ ... No, not her life. She'd wanted to breathe—it was breath she wanted—but different air—somewhere where fabric softener didn't rule—a vista without hills—with other hills—a new ecosystem—hers was clogged up. She wanted a history not written yet—she'd wanted to write it. She wanted to write.

2.

She wanted to keep what she loved close—she wanted to know what she loved. What she loved was green but another green—what she loved was behind her—also not here yet. What she loved was just out of reach—what she loved couldn't reach her and she hadn't reached it—she hadn't reached far enough—what she loved kept reaching out for her and she wanted some space—what she loved she wanted to ~~keep~~leave.

3.

She wanted fields—horizons—bounded by spiky bare trees—ideas—maybe a new degree. By degrees she left the horizons of home. She'd discovered herself on fire—burning down her life. She took off for the city—she took off her old face changed her hair left her house. She drove herself back and forth—she morphed. She wanted/was the whole of it, a galaxy. She wanted horizons. She wanted to give her children the world—she wanted the comets they had come to be to come back around—and they did—adults, frozen to her touch, their paths ablaze.

4.

What she wanted was home—to find it or make it—she wanted to give it back to herself—to claim what she loved. She came to it now where it always had been—in her arms—in her head—in her children, wherever she landed—horizons everywhere once she'd stopped spinning.

THAT'S GOOD

I do not know myself—I don't exist
to be known. Maybe I am here
only to pass along some genes. Resist
the temptation to believe there's more
than this, I tell myself some days. Love
the color of the sky, the crumpled leaf
stuck to your shoe. Be grateful you can move
these half-frozen knees. There's grief enough.
No need to finger every loss's gap
as if it were a missing tooth. No sprite
waits to swoop in with her gold. The lap
you long for is yours. Fold yourself right
in half, then reach. Lift someone else's ache
close. Inhale her scent. Give and take
comfort. There's nothing else. Later, some food,
maybe a bath, a place to sleep. That's good.

BEFORE THE BLOOM

The African violet cups itself—a satellite dish
arrayed toward waves, toward the tremble
of particles absorbed in velvet leaves. Just now
it isn't blooming and hasn't
for a while. I leave it
to benign neglect to keep from drowning it
in my need (to care for something
to feel real). It's not just the violet
who aims all her substance at what she requires.

On the messy shelf around the half-dead plant
a blue metal flower rises from a mossy stand
next to a clay angel. A small vase declares
"Friends for always." In a tooled leather frame
myself and the lifelong friend
who gave me flower, angel, vase.
Her mother raised huge violets
that did not have to lean into the sun,
that bloomed, pinks and whites
and blues in a quiet room I used to envy.
Orderly and well-fed, everything there.
I loved my friend for that rigorous peace

and love her now in spite of it. I know the cage
that order built. I'll keep
my chaos. Further down the shelf,
a half conch shell I picked up
the summer I'd lost a breast,
for its pink curve, its emptiness. Broken
as I was and as much itself.
Behind it a rank of journal books,
a hunk of pink amethyst a student gave me once

and feathers in an old ink pot. Maybe
I've squandered words and every
chance they might have shown me.
Maybe I ignored my own best interest,
overwatered what was dead.
I might have loved too hard and without order,

or maybe it took all of it to make a stem
tough enough to wait out the drought
that comes before the bloom.

QUESTION POEM
Poem for a Daughter
—*after May Swenson*

Daughter my river
my ocean my stone
who would I be
without your flowing

Where would I travel
How would I marvel
What would I treasure

Where could I hope
without your laughter
all ripple and flash
How would I know
in desert and drought
the promise of water
if Daughter your nimble heart's
wellspring was nowhere

How would it be
to travel unfettered
without love's sharp shaft
only thirst for a song

With hands empty and air
what would I carry?

EVICTION

Most of what
I lost I took
from myself.

THERE WAS A DOOR

There was a door and her hand
on its lever. In too many clothes—
her coat's wide cape collar,
her high button shoes, a bonnet
heavy and huge whose beruffled
lining frames a thin face.   Enough to smother a watcher.

For more than a century
she's stood, not going through.
Was she leaving or coming home?
Time has carried her cheekbones
into our Susie. Susie running
morning and evening,
as soon as she stood up to walk, she was
running.   I cannot imagine her

stopped so long in a doorway
in a browned bonnet, feet stilled
and buttoned, though the lattice
my grandmother stands at is the same
lattice on Susie's gate in Virginia.
Who made this photo? Maybe the door
isn't a door, though the ground's gritted
as if she were leaving   a garden.

What do I have to say today?
        Only Oh and Oh and Oh
let me cross my own boundary
        open the door—

or shut it if that's what it takes
to keep the dark out a while.
        Only a while, long enough

>   to open light's letter, to read
> the familial hand that is my hand
> open to draw me into the courtyard
>   out to the road.
>
> There was a door to the river
> I never lived beside—a door
> on its changing shoreline, its shining.
>   My hand on the lever.

II. Broken, Various, Inscrutable

THE NEXT KNOT

Untangle something small—a fine chain
retrieved from your drawer—something
you might put on again. Or perhaps the sheets
once you've made your clumsy exit into sunlight.
Smooth their tumble level as a lake.

Let motion itself take you into making
a pot of coffee or stacking yesterday's
dishes (the ones you
couldn't face).

The dishes waited. The weeds kept growing in the dark
while you slept. And the dog needs to pee.

Let him out. Take hold
of the lank stems crabgrass has wired into the ground.
Tug against what would take over. This is how
to loosen refusal's fist.

If you look up from the dog there is the fence,
and the next fence, the next—
the yards, linked like cells,
and the street that leads everywhere
and comes back to here. You don't have to go

everywhere. Only to the next place. The next
small act: the next knot
asking to be loosened
so the chain becomes itself again, beautiful
against the collarbone.

ANOTHER APRIL

> Maybe dying's like being given
> a box of what will be trumpets
>
> —Mark Doty, "A Box of Lilies"

And how were the trees at my mother's birth? In coves
along the muddy river when her mother
held her, newly sprung from the dark? All the unknown

swirls out from the two of them. None of it
what they imagined. The April day Mother died
down in Nashville, trees bloomed with a ferocious
hunger. The sky beat a burgeoning blue. "Maybe dying's
like being given a box of what will be trumpets,"
or so a poet said. "Maybe it feels like a mistake

and you plant them." Each of us opening—bulb
to blaring bloom, staining the noses of those who embrace us
with our pollen's lush desire to be carried forward.

Maybe we leave no more than this
bright orange emblem on the world—

though we pull everything into our brief
nectar's impossible sweetness.
Mother snug under April grass,
the blades thick and chill.
As if the soil could transport
anything other than a husk
through the zero of space,
whatever that means—

"space." Like clockwork,
this clicking onward, this ticking
of what we call time. What do I know?
Don't I wake up talking on to the dead? Don't I
orbit them still, these planets and suns? And our deaths?

Delivered unsought in a box, something we know
we didn't order—scaled bulbs nestled
in shredded brown paper, the diagnosis
flowering from the young cardiologist's mouth—
mere shaped breath and sound, words wet with
the damp of his living lungs, dispersing
as soon as they're spoken. But we've received them.

They've been delivered, an unwanted package
solid as lead at our center. It's April,

sunshine blows somewhere outside,
waxy leaves shove their green
up to the light. It's April. The dead wait
in gone kitchens, remembered yards,
holding our births, our deaths,
the whole of time in their timeless eyes,
at their feet lilies gather themselves to flare.

OUT THE DOOR

It's getting out the door that stands
between us and the world. I know. Open
the damn thing and step through. Broken
promises are all that hold us. Plans
we made and then ignored. The mess in the house
we're afraid will survive us. The quiet hours
we thought to have. Access to the powers
we felt as children, near in us, now lost
to lack of faith. The only thing that changes
is the heart. There's the door. The dream
kept the faith you dropped. Time arranges
more second chances than they tell us. Clean
breaks, old reservations waiting to be
taken up.

CONSIDER THE MEASURE OF A STEP

I.
Three feet
       at a time
              the world slips past—
every meter earned,

the weight of flesh and bone
our first burden.

To get anywhere,
an act of patience,
a job of work.

II.
Could I find that westward trail—the overgrown
       track—trace of the swale
those long gone wheels wore
       into sod?
Calculate the distance to the end of a continent.
By GPS it's only days—if you are able
          to plod without stop
              without rest
                    for your animal self
             without weather
                  washed out crossings.
To Oregon's undreamed orchards bent
        under the sweet cherries' weight
To California's strawberry fields
to the *other* forever picking there.

Hope, the truest mode of travel.

III.

It is one thing to set out.
          It is another to flee
         take flight.

Not light
            Not fit
    to journey.

         Hit
with missiles, metal messengers
you want to say have nothing
to do with your life.
             Lift
leaden feet.
     Flee.   Git.

IV.

               Even refugees,
carrying the nothing they still own,
carrying death in their sweat, death
haloing everything, can cross
the measure of entire countries
in days with no home
on the other end, no vision
of gardens, but mud and tents
waiting—and stasis and fences
erected to protect the dream
from them.

V.

What are the nights then?
        What darkness in the changing strange
                geography? What invasions
                of the no longer sovereign
bodies, riding the lurch and
            pitch of *La Bestia*, the sickening
       rise and ocean dip of an
            overcrowded raft.
The country of home
        a dream, a nightmare, a room
            never to be re-entered.
        The country underfoot forever
            foreign, no matter how much
            it was longed for. No matter
            how much it is loved.

VI.

I have not slept
along any of these roads. I have not
        fled one kind of destruction
        for another, not put myself
        in danger for a dream.
I haven't trudged—not on an asphalt edge not among rocks
                and wind, grit-driven, hot
                as a devil's breath, swelled
                with small clicks, the steps
                of predators. Nor have I shuddered
                into sleep on iron cold earth.
I have not stood for hours for a sack of meal,
        a plastic measure of tepid water.
I have not felt pure
        gratitude for a narrow cot,
            canvas overhead.

VII.

Today I have picked fruit out of season
from among a cool abundance
beneath the drift of sixties music.
Oregon cherries, a plastic measure
of California strawberries.

Today I have filled my car. Today I
have paid someone to guard
the borders. I have turned
the news off.

In a white bowl
on my table, berries
barely bruised.
On my fingertips
a tinge of red.

KNOBBED

Never a pretty season, spring, in those
barn lots, all red clay mud, hoof-pocked and draped
in the stench of manured straw. The stable's warm close
air spilled out with the ponies through the gaped
and hanging doors. Five mares, five tottery, knob-
kneed foals, who blinked and lifted pinpoint hooves.
The mares' winter-rough coats, all shag and rubbed-
bare spots, their legs mud-socked, so that they moved
in a slow, weighted dance—but it's the foals
I want to talk about—the huge knots
of their knees. How to reconcile
them with the slender too-long legs? And what's
more, with my own knees, my own ungainly gams?
And how we ran? How all of us fell back then and just
                                                  got up again.

STILL LONGING FOR THE DIVINE

Am I seriously looking for God again
—that cardboard figure of basement Sunday school
that three-faced sleight of spirit's longing
stirring me up, hushing me down?

Flicker of leaf in breeze, wink of windy starlight,
fingertip of water on the baby's forehead,
how I sang in Its imagined Presence
How His heat pulled life from my center

and let it fly out lusty as sunlight, simple as night.
Where is the dusty road gone? The place
where I followed His young Man? Foreign trail
familiar as the barn lane where we filmed

Saul's falling down into the light
wearing our striped bathrobes,
our towel head-dresses twisted like clumsy certainties
that kept unknotting even then.

Only Enormity left—leaf, star, a complicated
science—the soil teeming with alien life forms,
even my own skin not a simple wrapper,
not even only mine, but a shore

known to God's eye, revealed at last
by the electron microscope,
sustaining ancient essential creatures
crab-like, who creep the slender forests
of eyebrow, the plain of clavicle

clearing dead cell debris, part of me,
unwished for. God's light
broken, various,
inscrutable and lowly—

enfleshed in the ugly, the repulsive
beings who ride me as a planet.
And wasn't this what I was seeking all along,

this redemption?

POEM FOR A DAUGHTER, II

A whole new person grows inside her,
hidden. Not her. Smiling his secret smiles.
It's common as sunlight, this knitting together

of man and woman to fuse a fresh armature.
Desire's mitosis, the scaffolded cells—
Voila—a new person grows inside her.

Ready or not they've created a character
they can't control. Laundry and bills piled,
common as dirt. What they've started together,

focused or heedless, driven by pleasure,
reaches beyond them. Years and miles
later the person (who grew inside her)

will carry the print of them. And she's become Other,
Mother, a new kind of self. An exile
common as death, in thrall altogether

to what is not-her. Relentless surrender
pulls our flesh forward. The child's
his own person, moving inside her.
Common as diamonds, he knits them together.

MORTAL COIL

You wake up to
                  the room
      pivoting   the ceiling
tracing   slow   circles   overhead
         a carousel that won't   quite
                stop.

What is this flesh that it should
step between the morning light
and that joy you woke
to hold?

What coil of cartilage
    or bone, lovely
  as the sea
shell abandoned
             betrays the love
    that otherwise propels
  you out to see the sky?

Serpent in our garden, shine of dry scale,
flicker of divided loyalties—spirit tasting
sweet flesh, tart with longing,
over and over chooses

the mortal, the dizzying
ride into hope and loss,
this spinning place.

THANKSGIVING IN A YEAR OF FLOOD AND FIRE

> My heart is moved by all I cannot save;
> so much has been destroyed
>
> —Adrienne Rich, "Natural Resources"

My heart is moved by all I cannot save,
Adrienne said, and left us less alone.
My shattered heart regroups its parts, brave
for a moment in the face of all that's gone.
Age after age, perversely, she goes on,
we reconstitute the world. We put together pies,
we lose it on the phone, we call back to apologize,
broken by what we can't undo but on
the way (oh, let it be!) to doing something
good, even if it's only sweet
potato casserole again, the scalloped oysters
that our mother fixed. It's Thanksgiving,
feast of what never was, exactly. Its youngsters,
hungry for the future, clamor, "When do we eat?"

THE ABSENTEE NANA FIXES HER SOLITARY LUNCH

It has to be all of them—not just the oranges
though these are the sweetest ones in years
and not only the apple, though yesterday the apple

was plenty. No. Today it is everything
cut up. Everything! juicing the counter
and my arms, leaving a trail of peels and cores.

Grapefruit, blueberry, apple, the core-less
(not to be thought careless) banana,
and the too sweet to be believed

orange—bright orange cells, swelled
and tear-shaped, make me miss
everyone I love, miss fixing lunches
for someone other than myself. Blue,

red, banana ivory, grapefruit purple-pink.
I know how to get them—not the fruits,
the long gone daughters in their busy lives,

the grandchildren for whom my cooking
must be an acquired taste. Bright salad
in a clear glass bowl and homemade,

reheated chicken soup, thick with rice
and spinach. Which of the little ones
is it that hates greens? The closest

daughter's three hundred miles away
—too far for a photo-text to tempt—
and "Miss you so much. Mom" might
induce guilt. I hit delete
and eat it all myself.

OUR OWN

The insects are dying, so they say—*They*,
those Rachel Carson-types whose observations prey
on our 2 a.m. fears. In the insectless silence their insistent voices
thrum almost unheard—but there. You thought you had choices,
of what to believe, of what you called truth

but it's turning out (of course) that it's Earth
who has the last say. You wanted kids—
you would give them the world—that's what you said,
and you meant it. You wanted the asphalt, the houses,
the convenience of plastic, cheap travel, the gadgets. Now how is
this wrong? Abundance, getting our own—

don't we deserve it? Dominion, or at least a lawn
free of weeds or beetles. A clean world, one clear
of nuisance, of darkness, of pests.

Barren of everything dear.

WHAT DOES A HEAVEN REQUIRE?

1.
Could this be the Afterlife
              our ancestors dreamed?
After all, our flesh
is nothing more
than the soil they tilled,
the molecules of air they breathed—
reassembled.   What matter are we
           but theirs?

If the sum of this material world
holds true from the origin—
              nothing created or destroyed.
              Everything moving
              from form to form,

we are
an afterlife.

            2.

            Then what does *this* heaven
            ask of us?

Our hours,
the freedom from want
            some of us enjoy—
surely these are Eden's longed-for ease,
a paradise most on this planet can't conceive—or claim.

            And, Hell's alive here
            in prisons we erect—
            the skyless cells,
            the "fix" we have to have,
            no decent place we can
            afford to house ourselves.

        Still, some of us choose to live
        what looks like salvation
            locked away
                in gated enclaves,
                    bank accounts.
                            Among our own kind.

3.

Listen: Every living
                multicellular thing   every   complex being
    arose only after single cells embraced the alien:
                                    mitochondria!

                making this poem

as well as   cave art   chariots   bubble gum   spiked heels   Buicks
                                                    possible.

        A mesh of us and not-us.
        We're each a little cosmos.

What is the gut even now
        but upset,
            bereft of its essential microbes?
We sing our brief chemical chorus.
Cellular, transient,
        superior in no way
            to the planet's least particle.

DIORAMA

i.

All night I dream of running, the grass ardent green,
red at the roots, as if its cool blades veiled hot coals.
The world flaring up, burning down,
just as it's always done, and me
skimming along its top edge.
Running away from or to?
Saving something or someone,
showing my ass in the process—I wanted so hard

to do well—whatever it was I was doing—
learning to be old, flying a kite, holding the moon,
then letting her slide down my arm, drip off my fingertips
into the lightening sky. This morning it's blue,
whether I'm ready or not, my dreams

a country I've only heard of, never seen really—
except on tv,
which I'm keeping turned off,
though its news staggers toward me,
is already here,
never mind that I breathe in only birds at the feeder,
six purple finches come back. The grass I cross,
awake, is real, if curated,
turf coaxed and cared for by somebody
other than me.

ii.

In this instant's overlay here on this hilltop,
where horses not so lately grazed, I walk on the lost,
the layers, the neatly kept, disappeared fields,
their flicker of sunlight, whicker of mares nuzzling foals—
and below that, before the orderly farm, and in and around it,
thrushes and plovers and groundhogs and grass snakes

weave and dig and plait their places in meadows. They are not
here, those fences, those buildings, those mornings of walking out
to check on the stock, not them, not even the heavy arch
of dew-weighted grasses, the nodding of blossoms,
Queen Anne's lace, chicory, rooted in karst,
in the cave-riddled limestone still layered under
the YMCA, the Kroger, and us, and the cars
prowing the air still sleepy and slow, this Sunday morning,
on streets named for what is not there—"Old Field Way."
We wear our gym clothes, walk our dogs across a lost savannah.
It rolls out in its moment,
underneath this one—in copses of cane,

bottlebrush, bluestem,
bulrush and sedge, its birds
skimming the seeding abundance
I cannot conjure except as a faded,
stiff diorama,
where taxidermed buffalo,
shaggy with dust, lead
plaster "Indians"
toward painted horizons.

iii.

I can't find those neon grasses I ran through in sleep, icy-sharp
blades twisting out of the soil. I can't even find childhood's
winter rye, head-high in places, back in those Mays
when I lay caught in its whisper, in our side field
content in my creaturely skin. How I murdered
its perfect ocean of green, made my pathways
through broken stems, packed earth down behind me.
How I printed that world with my body,
in that other sunlight holding up nothing.

NIGHTS AT HOME AFTER THE SURGERY

In the dark in the days
after we return from surgery
the walls wait
I'm not sure what for.
But they are waiting
we are waiting

to not be shadowed
to not trip on the grotesque
apparition of what used to be

normal. The new heart
the heart new-made
learns at seventy

a new way to beat.
The lungs sink
under the weight
of scars and broken
sternum, under the memory

just out of reach—
of the bright place of knives,
the ventilator's push and hiss,
the constant sticks and pokes,
the sinking into nothingness.

What holds
us in place? What
brings the familiar
back to us from 2 a.m.'s

3-D dreams? The bookcase
watching watching.
The chair with its dark

presence there/not there.
The streetlight laying down
bands of darkness
through the blinds.

Your face shadow-strapped
to the pillow.

HOW TO GO ON

Someone is building a cardboard house
over a grate, an office building down the street,
a lean-to in a tent city, a backyard shed for mowers,
a room built of a gaze: two pairs of eyes, tented by a jacket
where two sleep on the ground—
(*Only one more night*, she whispers,
hoping that is true.) Someone
is picking up the pieces of the ruined house,
on the bombed street in Syria, in Baghdad,
in the Afghan village after the suicide bomb,
on an island after the storm.
But these are rocks
these thoughts, these fragments
of what I want to build. Of what was here,
is already here, is dreamed. The unbroken
sidewalk, the lighted window, the beds
not in metal cages, the table in a single
kitchen, the food on the plate. I am hoisting
one word at a time. I am speaking
to the ones in charge. I am saying—
So much suffering. We cannot uncause it.
But we can set ourselves to mend,
we can say, This is not the way to build
a world. I will pick up the rubble.
I will carry one stone at a time.

III. Unasked-for Singing

AFTER RAIN

Write it: The woman
gone to seventy saying
she will not
end up mad
at what she chose
She will
not raise walls
against possibility
against the self
walking across the creek bottom
after the night's hard rain
feet wet to the ankles
in the long grass
the fallen down house
lost to its own tumble
its single chimney standing
the rusted tap sticking up from bent weeds
promising clear water
past the tarnished flow
this thirst never quenchable
this shining

POEM WITHOUT A GAZELLE

Waiting for the doctor for a room the latest
test results for the iv nurse to finally
thread the catheter into the vein
so the test can start for the valet to find
and bring your car for today's exam to say
you're doing alright at least for your age
Waiting isn't how I planned to spend
these years but then when did my plans
shape what happened except maybe as rowing
against the tide might help a person land
somewhere downstream oh well a gazelle
had been scheduled to show up a few
lines back to fill the drab and empty
waiting room door but Nannette appeared instead
in cheerful printed scrubs to say you were okay
the test went well and you know her voice and face
did give off something of the veldt's sere grace.

ODE TO MY LEFT KNEE

who took me dancing
Wednesday night who leapt,
cavorted as though no one noticed—
O metal falseness, O invisible
prosthesis, O feared addition
to a scarred and scalpeled body,
I greet you with the first light,
warm under quilts and sheet,
testing my limbs.

    And O old severed knee
disappeared, who ran in pastures,
raced ahead and always fell
in the same spots—O knee I wore
until you would not work,
knee of blotched white scars
because I was that running child,
because in middle age
the chemo robbed
my feet of feeling
so still I fell and fell,
forgive me that I do not know
where they took you
when they sawed you off—
forgive your brutal and precise
excision, your no doubt
ignominious disposal.

        In some landfill
        or incinerator the ghost of you
        calls to my gone breast,
        the hips they took
        so I could walk again.

O knee of now, O dear flesh
rushing down Atlantic Avenue,
heedless, forgetting
to be grateful,
more than mere glue
and gravity must cause this flesh
to embrace you, this bone
to claim your joinery.

        O leg made new
and not without those weeks
of searing pain,
those days the body
tried to throw you out,
even as I sweet-talked you
"Be mine, be mine!"

    O healed knee, O
    mystery of the urge
    to be whole,
    if I am lucky
    I will wear you
    out as well. Huzzah!

NAMING IT

What murmuration of starlings screeches,
"Excuseme, imsorry forgivemeforcalling?"

What affliction, what scourge in their spangled feathers,
mobbing the feeder, filling the air with their call's rusty saws,

asks permission? Even the frivolous, drab mourning dove
hunkered down on the sill burbles her cosmic

license to fill up the air with transparent sound,
claim her cote, her place in the covey.

And that trembling of finches, dapper and raucous,
babble and fuss at the thistle, greedy, suspicious

as nursing home women, telling their lives
over and over, "Yes! This is what happened, it was this way."

Maybe today, part weather part creature, I'll practice appearing
—bird and tree, mess of feathers, crooked limb joints,

damp air and sharp beak, brimful with unasked-for singing.

POEM FOR A DAUGHTER, III

No snow today, no two below.
No diapers waiting in the pail for bleach.
No pail. No wooden house above the two-lane road,
no Freewill Baptist Church next door, no
cemetery on the point above our bedroom window.
No jewelweed, no damp dirt road rising in shade,
no poison ivy, no view of the Big Sandy as yet unseen
from the end of that trail. No weight, alive
in my arms, no new-broken ground thick with garden beans
wrapped in morning glory vines. Nothing twines here
except stillness broken by her call. They're not here
either, and yet
                    that baby and her daughter calling,
their tale about the broken washer fills the living room
with voices, brings back that forty-year-gone snow,
the smelly pail, the garden beans, the jewelweed.
Changed bodies—hers and mine—marked by births
and deaths, bad hips, a grandmother's imperfect
spine singing down the chromosomes. What isn't
here? What is? This August heat, cicada whir,
a cricket by the door, and everything unseen.

AT THE GATE

Say you are not watching people take off
their shoes, put their belongings on
a conveyor, empty their pockets
of change. Say you are wearing

an extravagant silk scarf,
oversized sunglasses, a brilliant
smile. No searches stand
between you and the silver

jet warming its engines
at the gate. But
no. The men keep
taking off their jackets,

the line inches forward,
all of us barefoot, bare
headed, heading toward
more lines, the roll call

at each gate. There is no
elegant scarf, only a lavender
cardigan. No sunglasses,
just your private smile

at your daughter
planning her wedding and
your same blessed husband
hours ahead. No movie Idlewild
departure, but KCI's concrete

terminal—an actual
ordinary   life.
    [wonderful]

THE WARP

Everything rusts, warps, settles off-center
askew. I ask you, Is *this* what I meant
to make of myself? Only, what entered
the cracks in the smooth façade of my intent
is bright—unforeseen as moonlight's
body in the radiant dark. Rusted solid,
I am stuck in spots I had set all my might
against, unaware when love's slow heat oxid-
ized me to what I said I didn't want.
Bent to the daily *make* and *keep* of mother, wife,
I thought myself a "shrinky-dink"—the life
baked out of me, my juices spent. What went
was only blinding rush and noise. I'll take
what's here—loss and what it made of me, what it let me make.

BETWEEN HEAVEN AND EARTH
On Falling at 67

"Knock yourself out!" they'll say when you ask permission.
Well, at least I didn't do that. I didn't ask and I did

remain conscious—but mostly of the strangeness.
That place between weightlessness and gravity,

the moment when your sense of balance deserts you
and you are suspended briefly. "Let go,"

they'll advise you when you're uptight.
It's that feeling of the world's hold on you

fleeing for once, though you know where you're headed,
and the reality is hard. "So far, so good," you'll think,

remembering the old joke: What did the guy say as he
passed the tenth floor on his way from ledge to sidewalk?

a line that's only funny in stand-up—
which you're not doing at the moment.

LADY PROTEUS

White-capped as wind-torn wave, I seem
to be mere restless motion, a late surge
of a graying sea. No sun gleam
breaks the choppy iron, nor sweet urge
brightens my steady beat toward a night
likely dismal cold. Shape-shifter, yes-
terday my sea sprang blue, a spritely
body, light and teasing, stealing treas-
ures from the hours. And before that,
I was fierce whirl, a water funnel whose spin took
everything into my momentary, urgent heart.
Stick skinny, I ran, I fell. I will not look
back except to claim the dances, the births
that grew and shrank me. That carry me to earth.

REINVENTION

What if everyone   let go at once
Put down the mop   closed his computer
threw the phone into the nearest toilet

took off the tie the heels   lay down hauled
comforter and pillow overhead
turned over on her side and sighed

Enough   Go away   How long
might we stay immobile   the mobiles shorted out
servers down   every screen
a faceless gray   tools resting where they lay

The force of let-out breaths   might well revive
old forests   give the tress some plain old food

for thought CO_2 minus particulates
of industry   Indolence all the rage
living our living   without wages

trading clothes for food   greetings for the news
A fool's paradise   Perhaps we'd all
be eaten alive   but not by avarice

or anxious striving   Time expanded   exponentially
without commutes deadlines   quotas   In the lull
someone pokes the soil   plants a bean   a flower
heads out to the shop   to reinvent

the wheel   Wouldn't someone somewhere spin
her poodle's hair to yarn   while her sister's
gone   up on the roof to scribble out

an ode   Meanwhile another's figured out
the sock and knits away   Or an old man takes
a notion he can organize a co-op   share the bounty

barters with the wheel guy to transport
sunflowers   socks   for rent and candle wax
A resurrected printing press clatters in a shed

A girl's wired up a light bulb   powered
by a stream   and someone's found a rock
that burns   set up a stand to sell the warmth
and soon   smoke has woken sleepers

Might as well give up on the bunch of us
We're here! We here! We won't
stop fixing making   cradles   ladles   coffee pots

A place not perfect   though it could be   if
we're careful   if we learn to pay attention
            good enough.

MORNING SHIFT WITH CANINE

Sometimes the simple rattle of a locust
in no particular tree will put the day
back on its feet, undo the night's tilt
into the grave. Some mornings an unfocused
August walk with the dog is all it takes.

Our bodies prow the sodden air—sun, spilt
through haze, legs churning. Sidewalk,
rank sod, the regular spaces at which he balks
next to the regular trunks, a chance to lift

our feet. We do this for each other—shift
our darknesses. I pick up his shit
and he, obligingly, takes mine, flings it
off his back paws. Each of us goes,
lightened, following his joyful nose.

SALT

Of course, we bear the loss
of anyone we love
as if only we could
know how loss

dismantles us. Of course
we're seized by giving
birth and for a while
live in that house,

as if no one else had
owned that space.
Even sore knees, hangnails
construct worlds

where we dangle,
cocooned in reverberations
only we can hear.

Everyone's hopes
—at last we see—
everyone's certainties
disintegrate in the daily

acid of revision.
The life we'd thought to lead
dissolved like so much salt.

What was it you thought
your tears bore away?

AND LUCKIER

> All goes onward and outward, nothing collapses,
> And to die is different from what any one supposed, and luckier.
>
> —Walt Whitman

It doesn't feel lucky, of course
—dying. Though now I've said it,
death wags her hoary noggin, slips
a grin into her skull, and
I can almost hear her *tsk tsk*
in a voice that is my grandmother's:
"You can't put an old head
on young shoulders," which

gets to mean something different
every year as this pate of pale
cornsilk, tawny waist-length, silvery-
streaked shoulder brushing, dyed bob,
white cap of hair rings its changes
on my crown. Different than what

we'd thought, for sure not the same
from under the cranium
that sported shining locks, glossy
and long as those summers
Dylans (Thomas, Bob) sang us
morning songs. Dead was dead.
The ultimate "unluck," stuck,

cut off from weather, friends,
the pleasure of the flesh
still keen, surely always keen.
And yet, death's wide face leans
over our sweet rest (when we can

find that), breathes close, hums, "Is this
so bad?" Sly mother of beauty,
that one. Siren. "Who knows

where we'll go. Summer of love?
Winter of discontent? You ain't
seen nothing yet." Oh, yes.

IN YOUR POCKET

Carry what you need, what
you need to hear—the poem
that says what must be
said that very moment: you are

alive, this is what it feels like
to be lost or found, to be a mother
watching her son, a father
whose jokes carry down
to the fifth generation. The pine
outside your back door never sang
in this wind until now. A yellow
bird never thrust its long bill
into the stump or flicked
the moss away until this hour,

teaching you its name. Carry the thing
you have to have to live. The stench of the wallow,
bouquets of honeysuckle, daisies,
and red clover, the hen's malevolent eye.

Tuck the dark into your shirt, let
the cat's rough tongue give you back
your childish fingers. No one but you
knows what you love.

WE ARE HERE

Time presses against the windows—
dark into daylight, daylight into dark again—
and you, changing—neap tide, spring tide,
ebb and rise. One year ago today you lay
in the ICU one day out
from the procedure—
open heart—that bought us
who knows how much time. One year
ago, I lay here longing only for the length
of you warm beside me in this bed—only
for the dark thinning as light slid in
to give me back the trees, the street,
the outline of a life.

This morning, we are here, slipping out of sleep.
I can reach you, touch your arm, the flesh between us
lax with age, and yet we make our way onto our feet,
into the day. Your breath rides its new rhythm,
my bones align themselves
to contain what time has given us.

ACKNOWLEDGMENTS

I am lucky to live and write in Lexington, Kentucky, a city with a vibrant and supportive literary community. Though writing is done in solitude, we writers need trusted readers to hear our words with that balance of celebration and critique that pushes the work toward what it can be. I am grateful particularly to these poet friends who read versions of both the individual poems and the manuscript in progress: George Ella Lyon, Sherry Chandler, Katerina Stoykova, Martha Gehringer, and Sue Churchill. In addition, I thank poets Marcia Hurlow, Kim Miller, Jeff Worley, and Susan Cobin—members of my longtime poetry group— who saw and shaped early versions of many of these poems. Thanks also, to Jan Isenhour, Gail Koehler, Susan C. Brown, Jan Walters-Cook, Marie Bradby, and Ann Olson for the space we've made, together, for writing— the space that allowed much of this work to come into being. And finally, a special thank you to Sherry Chandler whose keen mind, clear eye, and large heart never flagged as she read more versions of this collection than either of us care to number!

Thank you to the Carnegie Center for Literacy and Learning for creating programs that foster writers and the teaching of writing, for celebrating literature and its creation. I am grateful to the writers in my workshops and in the Author Academy: the courage and fearlessness of your writing never stops inspiring me. Some of these poems had their origins in our writing together.

Thank you to Lynn Winter—painter, writer, and person extraordinaire —for your spirit and presence and for the perfect cover art.

Huge thanks to Katerina and Accents Publishing who embraced *And Luckier*. Thank you for giving this book its best possible home. Katerina, you are a force of nature—and, of literature. I count myself among your lucky friends and admirers.

To Leslie and Micah, Eliza and Scott, Lyda and Darren—love and gratitude every day. And joy for Solly, Abie, Susie, and Nina, who hold the future. Most of all, thank you to my husband, Will—first reader, astute and gentle critic, whose steady encouragement has made all the difference. That day I first saw you in the doorway was the luckiest day of all.

The author gratefully acknowledges these journals in which the following poems have appeared, sometimes in slightly different form:

"That's Good," *Exit 7*

"Morning Shift with Canine," *Literary Accents*

"The Warp," "At the Gate," "Poem Without a Gazelle," "Poem for a Daughter, III," *Appalachian Heritage*

"Lady Proteus," *Passager Prize Issue*, 2019.

"The Next Knot," *Tar River Poetry*

"Your Fear," *Rattle Poets Respond*, December 21, 2018, https://www.rattle.com/respond/

"Another April," in slightly different form, *IWWG Journal*, 3rd place Myra Shapiro Poetry Prize

"Persephone Opens Another Bottle of Red," *New Madrid Review*

"Eviction," *See How We Are*, anthology, Accents Publishing

"Salt," the *James Dickey Review*

"Next World," as "Embryo," *Its Own Level*, anthology, Motifs Press

"Reinvention," *Appalachian Journal*

"The Absentee Nana Prepares Her Solitary Lunch," *Passager Prize Issue*, 2017

"House Beautiful," "In Your Pocket," *Still: The Journal*

ABOUT THE AUTHOR

Leatha Kendrick grew up on a southern Kentucky farm, daughter of a veterinarian and a high school home economics teacher. Oldest of four children, she was most at home in fields or barns (when not reading a book on the window seat and looking out at the horizon). Her adult life was spent in eastern Kentucky where she and her husband raised three daughters. Kendrick began writing seriously in midlife and found a first community of writers in Appalachia. Among her writing awards are two Al Smith fellowships from the Kentucky Arts Council, as well as the Sallie Bingham Award and fellowships and grants from the Kentucky Foundation for Women. Her poems, essays, memoir, and book reviews appear in journals including *Tar River Poetry*, *Appalachian Heritage*, *New Madrid Review*, the *Southern Poetry Review*, the *James Dickey Review*, *The Southern Women's Review*—and in many anthologies including *The Southern Poetry Anthology, Volume 3—Contemporary Appalachia*; *Listen Here!: Women Writing in Appalachia*; *I to I—Life Writing by Kentucky Feminists*; and *What Comes Down to Us—Twenty-Five Contemporary Kentucky Poets*. She currently lives with her husband and one lively small black dog in Lexington, Kentucky. *And Luckier* is her fifth collection of poems.

www.ingramcontent.com/pod-product-compliance
Lightning Source LLC
Chambersburg PA
CBHW030350100526
44592CB00010B/906